Atma Bodha

with an offering
of devotional hymns

First published by Mantra Books, 2012
Mantra Books is an imprint of John Hunt Publishing Ltd., Laurel House, Station Approach,
Alresford, Hants, SO24 9JH, UK
office1@jhpbooks.net
www.johnhuntpublishing.com
www.mantra-books.net

For distributor details and how to order please visit the 'Ordering' section on our website.

ISBN: 978 1 78099 398 0

A CIP catalogue record for this book is available from the British Library.

Printed and bound in the USA by Edwards Brothers Malloy

Atma Bodha

with an offering
of devotional hymns

Swamini Sri Lalitambika Devi

MANTRA
BOOKS

Winchester, UK
Washington, USA

CONTENTS

DEDICATION

The Lord is known through various names and forms to have myriad benevolent powers. So, the Lord is worshipped. Beyond the romance of devotional ritual, however, with its lamps, incense, petals, sweets, and love songs, all is one.

We can honor all forms of the Lord in each religion, as well as no name or form at all.

We can bow down to each being as an expression of transcendent truth.

In this way, we awaken.

Spiritual awakening brings peace to all. May we respect the earth as our mother, and all beings as our relations. May we share of our resources, so that the children grow up with enough to eat and access to education. May we live without the threat of violence. May we serve with compassion.

May all beings be liberated.

PART I:

Atma Bodha

Atma Bodha

For the seeker made pure
by the fire of devotion,
for the seeker whose desires
have been burnt to ash,
for the seeker
who shines with tranquility,
for such a seeker,
no longer distracted,
whose only prayer is to be free,
is this *Atma Bodha* composed. 1

There is certainly
no other way
than to know
through direct experience
that is beyond
the realm of the senses,
beyond
mind, intellect, or intuition.
Fire cooks food.
There is no more
immediate cause.
So, awaken.
Realize light,
and know *atman* in all. 2

Not incompatible with
binding action,
not causing
to cease
delusions of mind,
not halting the play
of knowledge and ignorance—
goodness is of the world
and a sibling to gloom. 3

Concepts of self
are limiting. Only
primordial light
destroys illusion.
Light shines forth
from within,
as if clouds had
passed
from the face
of the sun. 4

The soul
sullied by ignorance
becomes
extremely pure
through
study and practice.
What is learned
itself disappears,
as does the powder
of the *kataka* nut
that clears
muddy water. 5

Wandering lost in the world
of mind and body
is like living in a dream.
Desire and aversion
are as twins.
To be ruled by them
is to sleepwalk.
True light awakens. 6

Just as the glint
of an abalone shell
may be mistaken
for silver,
so the world of the senses
seems to shine.
Entranced,
one knows not
unalloyed
experience,
though all rests
in what is primordial. 7

The Lord[1] supports all.
The Lord is
like the pure gold
of which
alloyed ornaments
are created.
Created being
is an expression
of conscious
brilliance. 8

Space fills pots
of different shape
and size.
Like this,
the Lord dwells within
all created form.
Let limitations
be shattered,
and know yourself
to be whole. 9

Created being is varied,
though *atman*
is one in all.
As juice colors
and flavors water,
so qualities like
race, religion, and class
tinge the clarity
of being. 10

This body of earth,
water, fire, air,
and space
is an expression of
past action. Today's
pleasure and pain
are of ephemeral creation. 11

Vigour, along with
intellect, passion,
and sense experience,
compose the subtle body.
Discipline awakens one
to clear light. 12

Ignorance
of unexplainable beginning
shapes body and mind.
Three limitations—
physical, subtle, and causal—
are imprinted upon *atman*. 13

The soul in union
with the five
veils of illusion—
body, breath, emotion,
wisdom,
and bliss—
takes on
their characteristics,
as a piece of crystal
might appear
to be a sapphire
when placed upon
blue cloth. 14

Rice is threshed
to separate grain from husk.
So, through discernment,
break free from
the three limitations
and the five veils—
chaff. 15

Atman is
all-pervasive,
though not apparent
everywhere.
Clear consciousness
reflects it truly,
just as a clean mirror
reflects form
without distortion. 16

Many think the self
to be created
body, mind,
or even intellect.
This is confusion.
Know the still
inner witness.
Like a king,
atman
rules always
over creation. 17

Body and mind are
as ministers to the king.
They serve in the world,
while *atman*
remains unmoved.
The moon
appears to move
through the sky
when clouds scud.
So *atman* seems
to perform action,
though only body and mind
are in motion. 18

Actions of body
and mind depend
upon *atman*,
just as daily duties
can only be undertaken
by the light of the sun. 19

Not realizing *atman*,
most live deluded,
thinking the self
to be this
body and mind.
One might also
mistake the sky
for a finite blue dome,
though it is infinite space. 20

Confused,
a seeker lays claim
to action.
In the same way,
one sees
the reflection
of the moon's light
in water
and imagines that
the moon
itself moves
with the ripplings
of the river. 21

Passionate desire
brings joy and
sorrow.
These are of the mind.
Like dreams
that disappear
during deep sleep,
they vanish
with the rising light
of *atman*. 22

The sun is known
by its light.
Water cools.
Fire burns.
So *atman* is
experienced as
presence,
awareness,
and ecstasy—
the ever-stainless
atman. 23

I know, I need, I feel,
says the mind that is
mired in duality—
so unfulfilled
when not absorbed
in *atman*.
This confusion
brings about
birth after birth. 24

Mind is ever in flux.
Mind expresses itself
only by the light of *atman*,
though *atman*
knows no change.
How then does anyone live
in slavish ignorance
to mind? 25

Upon mistaking
a rope for a snake
in the dark,
the seeker is frightened.
So, one who confuses
the self with body and mind
is burdened by dread.
Know *atman*,
and become
fearless. 26

As planets
do not illuminate
the sun,
body and mind
shed no light
upon *atman*.
The light of
embodied *atman*
is like the flame
that shines
through the openings
of a lantern. 27

One who knows *atman*
desires no other,
just as a lighted lamp
is self-illuminating. 28

Be not bound
by false notion.
Not this. Not this.
The great truths
tell of union—
I am Brahman.
You are That.
This atman is Brahman.
Brahman is sheer ecstasy. 29

Identity is born of ignorance.
Body and mind
are like bubbles.
How easy it is to be free
of all that is ephemeral.
Know only,
I am Brahman,
effulgent and stainless. 30

I[2] am beyond creation.
Free am I of body and mind,
Unaffected am I by
birth, aging, illness,
or death.
These are of the body,
which I am not.
Neither do the senses
bring me pleasure or pain. 31

I am unmoved
by sorrow or joy,
dislike or hunger.
I know neither anger nor fear,
nor could I cling to another,
for all is in me,
and I am in all.
I shine. 32

From *atman* arise
breath, mind,
and sense experience.
So too come forth
the elements—
space, wind, fire, water, and earth.
Atman births the universe,
even as it conquers
attraction to creation. 33

I am not limited
by the science
of the natural world.
I am timeless,
simple, changeless,
beyond form,
and forever free. 34

I am like space.
I am everywhere,
within and without,
though I go nowhere.
I am the same in all,
perfectly fulfilled,
unattached,
and so of steady connection—
forever
resplendent. 35

Eternal, pure, and liberated,
I am.
I am whole—
an expression of truth[3]
without parts.
I am in ecstasy.
This being is one with all. 36

Turning within,
I inquire steadily
and merge.
To be as one
is the elixir
that heals worldly illness—
the sorrows of
a scattered mind
and its painful habits. 37

One who would merge
with truth
should find solitude and sit,
stoically conquering
all attraction,
to become one with *atman.*
Such boundless ecstasy
knows no other. 38

Created form dissolves into bliss.
One who yearns
becomes one with *atman*
and expands into space,
undisturbed and
limitless—
eternal. 39

Dropping ideas
of beauty, class, or creed,
one experiences
bare ecstasy—
the full perfection
of being. 40

To declare the knower,
knowing,
and the known
as one
asserts duality.
Atman is self-illuminating
and knows no such
distinctions. 41

In meditating
on *atman* alone
the flame of truth is kindled.
This sacred fire burns
desire to ash.
Action is purified. 42

As the light of dawn
rises
red in the east,
darkness is overcome.
So too, delusion
is swept away
when the light of *atman*
appears everywhere. 43

When *atman*
is steadily realized,
immature talk is silenced.
Awakening
to self-luminosity
is like suddenly remembering
the resplendent necklace
one has been wearing all along. 44

The mind that wanders
through the thicket
of ignorance
mistakes itself
for consciousness.
So, too,
one might behold
an inert tree trunk
in the dark
and think it a man. 45

As knowledge arises,
ideas of I and mine
are seen to be confused,
just as one notices
that the way
had been lost
during the night,
at sunrise. 46

The awakened one is present
throughout the universe.
One who looks with
the eye of wisdom
sees creation as *atman*—
the very self in all. 47

The universe is *atman*,
just as sundry pots
are all shaped from clay,
for there is none other
than *atman*.
One who looks deeply
into another sees
the self-same *atman*. 48

One touched by light
sees through former appearance.
The awakened one abandons
sloth, passion,
and even goodness
for true existence,
just as the cockroach
kissed by a bee
becomes itself,
a maker of honey. 49

Having crossed
the sea of enchantment
and slain
the demons of duality,
the awakened one is at peace—
merged
with the brilliance
of being. 50

The awakened one
loses interest
in external pleasure—
unsatisfying.
One liberated
is absorbed in
steady inner ecstasy
and shines
like a lantern,
lit from within. 51

One may inhabit a body
and also know truth.
The wise one,
rooted in mud,
is yet undisturbed
by the passions
of creation.
The sage walks the earth
freely,
as wind moves
through the sky.
The awakened one
is like the sky. 52

Limitations disappear.
The sage is not constrained
by body or mind,
but completely
lost in the Lord—
as water merges
into ocean,
air into sky,
and light into light. 53

That attained,
there is nothing left
to attain.
There is no
greater joy, and there is
nothing more to know.
Such is realization
of truth. 54

That seen,
all is seen.
Having become that,
there is no return.
Such is realization
of truth. 55

Above, below,
and all around
is pure
existence, awareness, and bliss.
Indivisible—
ecstasy is steady.
Such is realization
of truth. 56

Not these sheaths of
flesh or thought
is truth.
One who knows
truth intimately
experiences
no separation
or craving,
immersed
in the delight
of unending union.
Such is realization
of truth. 57

Ecstasy is not of form.
The savior is a small,
fleeting expression
of the whole. 58

In union with the whole,
become that essence.
Truth pervades ordinary
daily interaction,
while transcending all.
Truth is latent within,
as butter is in milk. 59

Not subtle, solid,
short, long,
unborn, imperishable,
formless, or of nature
is truth.
Such is true
realization. 60

Truth is the light
by which light shines.
Sun and moon
do not illuminate
primordial light,
but are themselves
lit by its splendor.
Such is realization
of truth. 61

Within, beyond,
and all throughout
shines truth.
Self-luminous, truth
lights the universe.
One who offers
this life to truth,
shines,
as a metal orb glows
in the heat
of fire. 62

Truth is distinct
from creation,
though it is
none other than this.
If anything is seen
to be other than light,
then what misperception—
a vision as unreal
as a mirage
in the desert. 63

Whatever is seen
or heard
or sensed in any way
is none other
than truth.
Awareness of truth
and truth itself
are not separate.
Truth is one
with existence,
consciousness,
and ecstasy. 64

Truth is everywhere,
though the ignorant
cannot perceive it,
just as one who is blind
does not see the brilliance
of the sun. 65

To hear of
and contemplate
truth
lights the flame
of wisdom.
The seeker
gives up impurity—
liberated,
like gold
that has released
its dross
into fire. 66

In the space
of the heart
arises *atman.*
Lustrous knowledge
drives off darkness.
Splendor pervades all,
supports all,
and simply shines. 67

Truth is of
primordial place
and time—
bright everywhere
without cause.
This heart
is the abode
of steady joy.
To know *atman*
is a kind of worship
that transcends ritual.
So, one awakens,
all-knowing
and pervading all,
having broken the bounds
of even death. 68

Such is the complete teaching
of Atma Bodha
composed by Sri Sankaracarya

Notes

[1]Visnu.

[2]The “I” refers not to the personal self, but to one in union with Brahman, or to that Brahman which is both immanent and transcendent.

[3]Brahman.

आत्म बोध

तपोभिः क्षीणपापानां शान्तानां वीतरागिणाम् ।

मुमुक्षूणामपेक्ष्योऽयम् आत्मबोधो विधीयते ॥ १ ॥

बोधोऽन्यसाधनेभ्यो हि साक्षान्मोक्षैकसाधनम् ।

पाकस्य वह्निवज्ज्ञानं विना मोक्षो न सिध्यति ॥ २ ॥

अविरोधितया कर्म नाविद्यां विनिवर्तयेत् ।

विद्याविद्यां निहन्त्येव तेजस्तिमिरसङ्घवत् ॥ ३ ॥

परिच्छिन्न इवाज्ञानात् तन्नाशे सति केवलः ।

स्वयं प्रकाशते ह्यात्मा मेघापायेंऽशुमानिव ॥ ४ ॥

अज्ञानकलुषं जीवं ज्ञानाभ्यासाद्विनिर्मलम् ।

कृत्वा ज्ञानं स्वयं नश्येज्जलं कतकरेणुवत् ॥ ५ ॥

संसारः स्वप्नतुल्यो हि रागद्वेषादिसङ्कुलः ।

स्वकाले सत्यवद्भाति प्रबोधे सत्यसद्भवेत् ॥ ६ ॥

तावत्सत्यं जगद्भाति शुक्तिका रजतं यथा ।

यावन्न ज्ञायते ब्रह्म सर्वाधिष्ठानमद्वयम् ॥७॥

सच्चिदात्मन्यनुस्यूते नित्ये विष्णौ प्रकल्पिताः ।

व्यक्तयो विविधाः सर्वा हाटके कटकादिवत् ॥८॥

यथाकाशो हृषीकेशो नानोपाधिगतो विभुः ।

तद्भेदाद्भिन्नवद्भाति तन्नाशे केवलो भवेत् ॥९॥

नानोपाधिवशादेव जातिवर्णाश्रमादयः ।

आत्मन्यारोपितास्तोये रसवर्णादि भेदवत् ॥१०॥

पञ्चीकृतमहाभूतसम्भवं कर्मसञ्चितम् ।

शरीरं सुखदुःखानां भोगायतनमुच्यते ॥११॥

पञ्चप्राणमनोबुद्धिदशेन्द्रियसमन्वितम् ।

अपञ्चीकृतभूतोत्थं सूक्ष्माङ्गं भोगसाधनम् ॥१२॥

अनाद्यविद्यानिर्वाच्या कारणोपाधिरुच्यते ।

उपाधित्रितयादन्यम् आत्मानमवधारयेत् ॥१३॥

पञ्चकोशादियोगेन तत्तन्मय इव स्थितः ।

शुद्धात्मा नीलवस्त्रादियोगेन स्फटिको यथा ॥१४॥

वपुस्तुषादिभिः कोशैर्युक्तं युक्त्यवघाततः ।

आत्मानमन्तरं शुद्धं विविच्यात्तण्डुलं यथा ॥१५॥

सदा सर्वगतोऽप्यात्मा न सर्वत्रावभासते ।

बुद्धावेवावभासेत स्वच्छेषु प्रतिबिम्बवत् ॥१६॥

देहेन्द्रियमनोबुद्धिप्रकृतिभ्यो विलक्षणम् ।

तद्वृत्तिसाक्षिणं विद्याद् आत्मानं राजवत्सदा ॥१७॥

व्यापृतेष्विन्द्रियेष्वात्मा व्यापारीवाविवेकिनाम् ।

दृश्यतेऽभ्रेषु धावत्सु धावन्निव यथा शशी ॥१८॥

आत्मचैतन्यमाश्रित्य देहेन्द्रियमनोधियः ।

स्वक्रियार्थेषु वर्तन्ते सूर्यालोकं यथा जनाः ॥१९॥

देहेन्द्रियगुणान् कर्माण्यमले सच्चिदात्मनि ।

अध्यस्यन्त्यविवेकेन गगने नीलतादिवत् ॥२०॥

अज्ञानान्मानसोपाधेः कर्तृत्वादीनि चात्मनि ।

कल्प्यन्तेऽम्बुगते चन्द्रे चलनादि यथाम्भसः ॥२१॥

रागेच्छासुखदुःखादि बुद्धौ सत्यां प्रवर्तते ।

सुषुप्तौ नास्ति तन्नाशे तस्माद्बुद्धेस्तु नात्मनः ॥२२॥

प्रकाशोऽर्कस्य तोयस्य शैत्यमग्नेर्यथोष्णता ।

स्वभावः सच्चिदानन्दनित्यनिर्मलतात्मनः ॥२३॥

आत्मनः सच्चिदंशश्च बुद्धेर्वृत्तिरिति द्वयम् ।

संयोज्य चाविवेकेन जानामीति प्रवर्तते ॥२४॥

आत्मनो विक्रिया नास्ति बुद्धेर्बोधो न जात्विति ।

जीवः सर्वमलं ज्ञात्वा ज्ञाता द्रष्टेति मुह्यति ॥२५॥

रज्जुसर्पवदात्मानं जीवं ज्ञात्वा भयं वहेत् ।

नाहं जीवः परात्मेति ज्ञातश्चेन्निर्भयो भवेत् ॥२६॥

आत्मावभासयत्येको बुद्ध्यादीनीन्द्रियाण्यपि ।

दीपो घटादिवत्स्वात्मा जडैस्तैर्नावभास्यते ॥२७॥

स्वबोधे नान्यबोधेच्छा बोधरूपतयात्मनः ।

न दीपस्यान्यदीपेच्छा यथा स्वात्मप्रकाशने ॥२८॥

निषिध्य निखिलोपाधीन् नेति नेतीति वाक्यतः ।

विद्यादैक्यं महावाक्यैर्जीवात्मपरमात्मनोः ॥२९॥

आविद्यकं शरीरादि दृश्यं बुद्बुदवत्क्षरम् ।

एतद्विलक्षणं विद्याद् अहं ब्रह्मेति निर्मलम् ॥३०॥

देहान्यत्वान्नमे जन्मजराकार्श्यलयादयः ।

शब्दादिविषयैः सङ्गो निरिन्द्रियतया न च ॥३१॥

अमनस्त्वान्न मे दुःखरागद्वेषभयादयः ।

अप्राणो ह्यमनाः शुभ्र इत्यादि श्रुतिशासनात् ॥३२॥

एतस्माज्जायते प्राणो मनः सर्वेन्द्रियाणि च ।

खं वायुर्ज्योतिरापः पृथिवी विश्वस्य धारिणी ॥३३॥

निर्गुणो निष्क्रियो नित्यो निर्विकल्पो निरञ्जनः ।

निर्विकारो निराकारो नित्यमुक्तोऽस्मि निर्मलः ॥३४॥

अहमाकाशवत्सर्वं बहिरन्तर्गतोऽच्युतः ।

सदा सर्वसमः सुद्धो निस्सङ्गो निर्मलोऽचलः ॥३५॥

नित्यशुद्धविमुक्तैकम् अखण्डानन्दमद्वयम् ।

सत्यं ज्ञानमनन्तं यत् परं ब्रह्माहमेव तत् ॥३६॥

एवं निरन्तराभ्यास ब्रह्मैवास्मीति वासना ।

हरत्यविद्याविक्षेपान् रोगानिव रसायनम् ॥३७॥

विविक्तदेशे आसीनो विरागो विजितेन्द्रियः ।

भावयेदेकमात्मानं तमनन्तमनन्यधीः ॥३८॥

आत्मन्येवाखिलं दृश्यं प्रविलाप्य धिया सुधीः ।

भावयेदेकमात्मानं निर्मलाकाशवत्सदा ॥३९॥

रूपवर्णादिकं सर्वं विहाय परमार्थवित् ।

परिपूर्णचिदानन्दस्वरूपेणावतिष्ठते ॥४०॥

ज्ञातृज्ञानज्ञेयभेदः परे नात्मनि विद्यते ।

चिदानन्दैकरूपत्वाद् दीप्यते स्वयमेव तत् ॥४१॥

एवमात्मारणौ ध्यानमथने सततं कृते ।

उदितावगतिर्ज्वाला सर्वाज्ञानेन्धनं दहेत् ॥ ४२ ॥

अरुणेनेव बोधेन पूर्वं सन्तमसे हृते ।

तत आविर्भवेदात्मा स्वयमेवांशुमानिव ॥ ४३ ॥

आत्मा तु सततं प्राप्तोऽप्यप्राप्तवदविद्यया ।

तन्नाशे प्राप्तवद्भाति स्वकण्ठाभरणं यथा ॥ ४४ ॥

स्थाणौ पुरुषवद् भ्रान्त्या कृता ब्रह्मणि जीवता ।

जीवस्य तात्त्विके रूपे तस्मिन्दृष्टे निवर्तते ॥ ४५ ॥

तत्त्वस्वरूपानुभवाद् उत्पन्नं ज्ञानमञ्जसा ।

अहं ममेति चाज्ञानं बाधते दिग्भ्रमादिवत् ॥ ४६ ॥

सम्यग्विज्ञानवान् योगी स्वात्मन्येवाखिलं जगत् ।

एकं च सर्वमात्मानम् ईक्षते ज्ञानचक्षुषा ॥ ४७ ॥

आत्मैवेदं जगत्सर्वम् आत्मनोऽन्यन्न विद्यते ।

मृदो यद्वद्घटादीनि स्वात्मानं सर्वमीक्षते ॥ ४८ ॥

जीवन्मुक्तस्तु तद्विद्वान् पूर्वोपाधिगुणांस्त्यजेत् ।

सच्चिदानन्दरूपत्वाद् भवेद्भ्रमरकीटवत् ॥४९॥

तीर्त्वा मोहार्णवं हत्वा रागद्वेषादिराक्षसान् ।

योगी शान्तिसमायुक्त आत्मारामो विराजते ॥५०॥

बाह्यानित्यसुखासक्तिं हित्वात्मसुखनिर्वृतः ।

घटस्थदीपवत्स्वस्थः स्वान्तरेव प्रकाशते ॥५१॥

उपाधिस्थोऽपि तद्धर्मैरलिप्तो व्योमवन्मुनिः ।

सर्वविन्मूढवत्तिष्ठेद् असक्तो वायुवच्चरेत् ॥५२॥

उपाधिविलयाद्विष्णौ निर्विशेषं विशेन्मुनिः ।

जले जलं वियद्व्योम्नि तेजस्तेजसि वा यथा ॥५३॥

यल्लाभान्नापरो लाभो यत्सुखान्नापरं सुखम् ।

यज्ज्ञानान्नापरं ज्ञानं तद्ब्रह्मेत्यवधारयेत् ॥५४॥

यद्दृष्ट्वा नापरं दृश्यं यद्भूत्वा न पुनर्भवः ।

यज्ज्ञात्वा नापरं ज्ञेयं तद्ब्रह्मेत्यवधारयेत् ॥५५॥

तिर्यगूर्ध्वमधः पूर्णं सच्चिदानन्दमद्वयम् ।

अनन्तं नित्यमेकं यत् तद्ब्रह्मेत्यवधारयेत् ॥५६॥

अतद्व्यावृत्तिरूपेण वेदान्तैर्लक्ष्यतेऽद्वयम् ।

अखण्डानन्दमेकं यत् तद्ब्रह्मेत्यवधारयेत् ॥५७॥

अखण्डानन्दरूपस्य तस्यानन्दलवाश्रिताः ।

ब्रह्माद्यास्तारतम्येन भवन्त्यानन्दिनोऽखिलाः ॥५८॥

तद्युक्तमखिलं वस्तु व्यवहारस्तदन्वितः ।

तस्मात्सर्वगतं ब्रह्म क्षीरे सर्पिरिवाखिले ॥५९॥

अनण्वस्थूलमह्रस्वम् अदीर्घमजमव्ययम् ।

अरूपगुणवर्णाख्यं तद्ब्रह्मेत्यवधारयेत् ॥६०॥

यद्भासा भास्यतेऽर्कादि भास्यैर्यत्तु न भास्यते ।

येन सर्वमिदं भाति तद्ब्रह्मेत्यवधारयेत् ॥६१॥

स्वयमन्तर्बहिर्व्याप्य भासयन्नखिलं जगत् ।

ब्रह्म प्रकाशते वह्निप्रतप्तायसपिण्डवत् ॥६२॥

जगद्विलक्षणं ब्रह्म ब्रह्मणोऽन्यन्न किञ्चन ।

ब्रह्मान्यद्भाति चेन्मिथ्या यथा मरुमरीचिका ॥ ६३ ॥

दृश्यते श्रूयते यद्यद् ब्रह्मणोऽन्यन्न तद्भवेत् ।

तत्त्वज्ञानाच्च तद्ब्रह्म सच्चिदानन्दमद्वयम् ॥ ६४ ॥

सर्वगं सच्चिदानन्दं ज्ञानचक्षुर्निरीक्षते ।

अज्ञानचक्षुर्नेक्षेत भास्वन्तं भानुमन्धवत् ॥ ६५ ॥

श्रवणादिभिरुद्दीप्तज्ञानाग्निपरितापितः ।

जीवः सर्वमलान्मुक्तः स्वर्णवद्द्योतते स्वयम् ॥ ६६ ॥

हृदाकाशोदितो ह्यात्मा बोधभानुस्तमोऽपहृत् ।

सर्वव्यापी सर्वधारी भाति भासयतेऽखिलम् ॥ ६७ ॥

दिग्देशकालाद्यनपेक्ष्य सर्वगं शीतादिहृन्नित्यसुखं निरञ्जनम् ।

यस्स्वात्मतीर्थं भजते विनिष्क्रियः स सर्ववित्सर्वगतोऽमृतो भवेत् ॥ ६८ ॥

॥ इति श्रीशङ्कराचार्यविरचित आत्मबोधः सम्पूर्णः ॥

ātma bodha

tapobhiḥ kṣīṇa-pāpānāṁ śāntānāṁ vīta-rāgiṇām,
mumukṣūṇām apekṣyo'yam ātma-bodho vidhīyate. 1

bodho'nya-sādhanebhyo hi sākṣān mokṣaika-sādhanam,
pākasya vahnivaj jñānaṁ vinā mokṣo na sidhyati. 2

avirodhitayā karma nāvidyāṁ vinivartayet,
vidyāvidyāṁ nihantyeva tejas timira-saṅghavat. 3

paricchinna ivājñānāt tan-nāśe sati kevalaḥ,
svayaṁ prakāśate hyātmā meghāpāyeṁ'śumān iva. 4

ajñāna-kaluṣaṁ jīvaṁ jñānābhyāsād vinirmalam,
kṛtvā jñānaṁ svayaṁ naśyej jalaṁ kataka-reṇuvat. 5

saṁsāraḥ svapna-tulyo hi rāga-dveṣādi-saṅkulaḥ,
sva-kāle satyavad-bhāti prabodhe satyasad bhavet. 6

tāvat satyaṁ jagad bhāti śuktikā-rajataṁ yathā,
yāvan na jñāyate brahma sarvādhiṣṭhānam advayam. 7

sac-cid-ātmanyanusyūte nitye viṣṇau prakalpitāḥ,
vyaktayo vividhāḥ sarvā hāṭake kaṭakādivat. 8

yathākāśo hṛṣīkeśo nānopādhi-gato vibhuḥ,
tad-bhedād bhinnavad bhāti tan-nāśe kevalo bhavet. 9

nānopādhi-vaśād eva jāti-varṇāśramādayaḥ,
ātmanyāropitās toye rasa-varṇādi bhedavat. 10

pañcī-kṛta-mahā-bhūta sambhavaṁ karma-sañcitam,
śarīraṁ sukha-duḥkhānāṁ bhogāyatanam ucyate. 11

pañca-prāṇa-mano-buddhi daśendriya-samanvitam,
apañcī-kṛta-bhūtotthaṁ sūkṣmāṅgaṁ bhoga-sādhanam. 12

anādya vidyānirvācyā kāraṇopādhir ucyate,
upādhi-tritayād anyam ātmānam avadhārayet. 13

pañca-kośādi-yogena tat tanmaya iva sthitaḥ,
śuddhātmā nīla-vastrādi-yogena sphaṭiko yathā. 14

vapus-tuṣādibhiḥ kośair yuktaṁ yuktya vaghātataḥ,
ātmānam antaraṁ śuddhaṁ vivicyāt taṇḍulaṁ yathā. 15

sadā sarva gato'pyātmā na sarvatrāvabhāsate,
buddhāvevāvabhāseta svaccheṣu pratibimbavat. 16

dehendriya-mano-buddhi-prakṛtibhyo vilakṣaṇam,
tad-vṛtti-sākṣiṇaṁ vidyād ātmānaṁ rājavat sadā. 17

vyāpṛteṣvindriyeṣvātmā vyāpārīvāvivekinām,
dṛśyate'bhreṣu dhāvatsu dhāvanniva yathā śaśī. 18

ātma-caitanyam āśritya dehendriya-mano-dhiyaḥ,
sva-kriyārtheṣu vartante sūryālokaṁ yathā janāḥ. 19

dehendriya-guṇān karmāṇyamale sac-cid-ātmani,
adhyasyantyavivekena gagane nīlatādivat. 20

ajñānān mānasopādheḥ kartṛtvādīni cātmani,
kalpyante'mbu-gate candre calanādi yathāmbhasaḥ. 21

rāgecchā-sukha-duḥkhādi buddhau satyāṁ pravartate,
suṣuptau nāsti tan-nāśe tasmād buddhes tu nātmanaḥ. 22

prakāśo'rkasya toyasya śaityam agner yathoṣṇatā,
sva-bhāvaḥ sac-cid-ānanda-nitya-nirmalatātmanaḥ. 23

tmanaḥ sac-cid-aṁśaś ca buddher vṛttir iti dvayam,
saṁyojya cāvivekena jānāmīti pravartate. 24

ātmano vikriyā nāsti buddher bodho na jātviti,
jīvaḥ sarvamalaṁ jñātvā jñātā draṣṭeti muhyati. 25

rajju-sarpavad ātmānaṁ jīvaṁ jñātvā bhayaṁ vahet,
nāhaṁ jīvaḥ parātmeti jñātaścen nirbhayo bhavet. 26

ātmā vabhāsayatyeko buddhyādīnīndriyāṇyapi,
dīpo ghaṭādivatsvātmā jaḍais tair nāvabhāsyate. 27

sva-bodhe nānya-bodhecchā bodha-rūpatayātmanaḥ,
na dīpasyānya-dīpecchā yathā svātma-prakāśane. 28

niṣidhya nikhilopādhīn neti netīti vākyataḥ,
vidyād aikyaṁ mahā-vākyair jīvātma-paramātmanoḥ. 29

āvidyakaṁ śarīrādi dṛśyaṁ budbudavat kṣaram,
etad-vilakṣaṇaṁ vidyād ahaṁ brahmeti nirmalam. 30

dehānyatvān na me janma-jarā-kārśya-layādayaḥ,
śabdādi-viṣayaiḥ saṅgo nirindriyatayā na ca. 31

amanastvān na me duḥkha-rāga-dveṣa-bhayādayaḥ,
aprāṇo hyamanāḥ śubhra ityādi śruti-śāsanāt. 32

etasmāj jāyate prāṇo manaḥ sarvendriyāṇi ca,
khaṁ vāyur jyotir āpaḥ pṛthivī viśvasya dhāriṇī. 33

nirguṇo niṣkriyo nityo nirvikalpo nirañjanaḥ,
nirvikāro nirākāro nitya-mukto'smi nirmalaḥ. 34

aham ākāśavat sarvaṁ bahir-antar-gato'cyutaḥ,
sadā sarva-samaḥ suddho nissaṅgo nirmalo'calaḥ. 35

nitya-śuddha-vimuktaikam akhaṇḍānandam advayam,
satyaṁ jñānam anantaṁ yat paraṁ brahmāham eva tat. 36

evaṁ nirantarābhyāsa brahmaivāsmīti vāsanā,
haratyavidyā-vikṣepān rogān iva rasāyanam. 37

vivikta-deśe āsīno virāgo vijitendriyaḥ,
bhāvayed ekam ātmānaṁ tam anantam ananya-dhīḥ. 38

ātmanyevākhilaṁ dṛśyaṁ pravilāpya dhiyā sudhīḥ,
bhāvayed ekam ātmānaṁ nirmalākāśavatsadā. 39

rūpa-varṇādikaṁ sarvaṁ vihāya paramārtha-vit,

paripūrṇa-cid-ānanda-sva-rūpeṇāvatiṣṭhate. 40

jñātṛ-jñāna-jñeya-bhedaḥ pare nātmani vidyate,

cid-ānandaika-rūpatvād dīpyate svayam eva tat. 41

evam ātmāraṇau dhyāna-mathane satataṁ kṛte,

uditāvagatir jvālā sarvājñānendhanaṁ dahet. 42

aruṇeneva bodhena pūrvaṁ santamase hṛte,

tata āvir-bhaved ātmā svayam evāṁśumān iva. 43

ātmā tu satataṁ prāpto'pyaprāptavad avidyayā,

tan-nāśe prāptavad bhāti sva-kaṇṭhābharaṇaṁ yathā. 44

sthāṇau puruṣavad bhrāntyā kṛtā brahmaṇi jīvatā,

jīvasya tāttvike rūpe tasmin dṛṣṭe nivartate. 45

tattva-sva-rūpānubhavād utpannaṁ jñānam-añjasā,

ahaṁ mameti cājñānaṁ bādhate dig-bhramādivat. 46

samyag-vijñānavān yogī svātmanyevākhilaṁ jagat,

ekaṁ ca sarvam ātmānam īkṣate jñāna-cakṣuṣā. 47

ātmaivedaṁ jagat sarvam ātmano'nyan na vidyate,
mṛdo yadvad ghaṭādīni svātmānaṁ sarvam īkṣate. 48

jīvan-muktas tu tad-vidvān pūrvopādhi-guṇāṁs tyajet,
sac-cid-ānanda-rūpatvād bhaved bhramara kīṭavat. 49

tīrtvā mohārṇavaṁ hatvā rāga-dveṣādi-rākṣasān,
yogī śānti-samāyukta ātmārāmo virājate. 50

bāhyānitya sukhāsaktiṁ hitvātma sukha-nirvṛtaḥ,
ghaṭa-stha-dīpavat sva-sthaḥ svāntar eva prakāśate. 51

upādhi-stho'pi tad-dharmair alipto vyomavan muniḥ,
sarva-vin mūḍhavat tiṣṭhed asakto vāyuvac caret. 52

upādhi-vilayād viṣṇau nirviśeṣaṁ viśen muniḥ,
jale jalaṁ viyad vyomni tejas tejasi vā yathā. 53

yallābhān nāparo lābho yat-sukhān nāparaṁ sukham,
yaj-jñānān nāparaṁ jñānaṁ tad brahmetyavadhārayet. 54

yad dṛṣṭvā nāparaṁ dṛśyaṁ yad bhūtvā na punar-bhavaḥ,
yaj jñātvā nāparaṁ jñeyaṁ tad brahmetyavadhārayet. 55

tiryag ūrdhvam adhaḥ pūrṇaṁ sac-cid-ānandam advayam,
anantaṁ nityam ekaṁ yat tad brahmetyavadhārayet. 56

atad-vyāvṛtti-rūpeṇa vedāntair lakṣyate'dvayam,
akhaṇḍānandam ekaṁ yat tad brahmetyavadhārayet. 57

akhaṇḍānanda-rūpasya tasyānanda-lavāśritāḥ,
brahmādyās tāra-tamyena bhavantyānandino'khilāḥ. 58

tad-yuktam akhilaṁ vastu vyavahāras tad-anvitaḥ,
tasmāt sarva-gataṁ brahma kṣīre sarpir ivākhile. 59

anaṇvasthūlam ahṛsvam adīrgham ajam avyayam,
arūpa-guṇa-varṇākhyaṁ tad brahmetyavadhārayet. 60

yad-bhāsā bhāsyate'rkādi bhāsyair yat tu na bhāsyate,
yena sarvam idaṁ bhāti tad brahmetyavadhārayet. 61

svayam antar-bahir vyāpya bhāsayannakhilaṁ jagat,
brahma prakāśate vahni-prataptāyasa piṇḍavat. 62

jagad-vilakṣaṇaṁ brahma brahmaṇo'nyan na kiñcana,
brahmānyad bhāti cen mithyā yathā maru-marīcikā 63

dṛśyate śrūyate yad yad brahmaṇo'nyan na tad bhavet,

tattva-jñānāc ca tad brahma sac-cid-ānandam advayam. 64

sarvagaṁ sac-cid-ānandaṁ jñāna-cakṣur nirīkṣate,

ajñāna-cakṣur nekṣeta bhāsvantaṁ bhānum andhavat. 65

śravaṇādibhir uddīpta-jñānāgni paritāpitaḥ,

jīvaḥ sarva-malān muktaḥ svarṇavad dyotate svayam. 66

hṛd-ākāśodito hyātmā bodha-bhānus tamo'pahṛt,

sarva-vyāpī sarva-dhārī bhāti bhāsayate'khilam. 67

dig-deśa-kālādyanapekṣya sarvagaṁ

śītādi-hṛn nitya-sukhaṁ nirañjanam,

yassvātma-tīrthaṁ bhajate viniṣkriyaḥ

sa sarva-vit sarva-gato'mṛto bhavet. 68

iti śrī-śaṅkarācārya-viracita ātma-bodhaḥ sampūrṇaḥ

PART II:

Devotional Hymns

Bhaja Govindam

Love the Lord, love the Lord.
The Lord—
love him, bewildered one.
You of foolish resolve,
memorizing and reciting
the rules of grammar
is no match for death.
When the time comes
rote
discipline
will not free you. 1

You gone astray,
give up
dogged repetition
of another's words.
Let the thirst
for wealth and pleasure
be slaked like this:
Contemplate your deeds.
Accept
what is now.
Devote yourself
completely
to knowing the Lord. 2

Love the Lord, love the Lord.
The Lord—
love him, bewildered one.
You of foolish resolve,
memorizing and reciting
the rules of grammar
is no match for death.
At the appointed time
rote
discipline
will not free you.

Entranced
by worldly love,
stand strong.
Attraction to flesh
is delusion.
Resist the uprising
of desire.
Choose to know
the Lord alone. 3

Love the Lord, love the Lord.
The Lord—
love him, bewildered one.
You of foolish resolve,
memorizing and reciting
the rules of grammar
is no match for death.
At the appointed time
rote
discipline
will not free you.

A water droplet trembles
against the lotus petal.
So, too, the
bound soul
may be unsure
in this world of
desire,
pride,
and sorrow.
Stay even-minded. 4

Love the Lord, love the Lord.
The Lord—
love him, bewildered one.
You of foolish resolve,
memorizing and reciting
the rules of grammar
is no match for death.
At the appointed time
rote
discipline
will not free you.

With your youthful
hands full of riches,
so will worldly
loved ones stay true,
but no one in the house
cares to speak
to one who is
old, feeble,
and forgotten. 5

Love the Lord, love the Lord.
The Lord—
love him, bewildered one.
You of foolish resolve,
memorizing and reciting
the rules of grammar
is no match for death.
At the appointed time
rote
discipline
will not free you.

While the breath
makes its home
in the body,
the family kindly inquires,
caring for you—
but when the breath
departs, even
your dearest
will turn away
from the corpse. 6

Love the Lord, love the Lord.
The Lord—
love him, bewildered one.
You of foolish resolve,
memorizing and reciting
the rules of grammar
is no match for death.
At the appointed time
rote
discipline
will not free you.

A child plays.
Youth clings
to the beauty
of another.
One who is grown,
mature,
gets lost
in worry.
When are we
ever
so absorbed
in the Lord? 7

Love the Lord, love the Lord.
The Lord—
love him, bewildered one.
You of foolish resolve,
memorizing and reciting
the rules of grammar
is no match for death.
At the appointed time
rote
discipline
will not free you.

Who truly
is your most beloved?
Who is your child?
Family bonds bewilder.
To whom do you
belong, and from where
did you come?
Ponder it deeply, now—
for you are my kin. 8

Love the Lord, love the Lord.
The Lord—
love him, bewildered one.
You of foolish resolve,
memorizing and reciting
the rules of grammar
is no match for death.
At the appointed time
rote
discipline
will not free you.

In the company
of the wise,
forget
worldly attachment.
When fleeting pleasure
and pain
are renounced,
so are we freed
from delusion.
Free of delusion,
the mind steadies.
With mind lost
in the Lord,
the soul is liberated. 9

Love the Lord, love the Lord.
The Lord—
love him, bewildered one.
You of foolish resolve,
memorizing and reciting
the rules of grammar
is no match for death.
At the appointed time
rote
discipline
will not free you.

When youthful vigor
is outgrown,
who feels lust?
When the lakebed is dry,
where are
the playful waters?
With all wealth spent,
can our loved ones
be sated?
When the knower goes
beyond all this,
who is left
to experience sorrow? 10

Love the Lord, love the Lord.
The Lord—
love him, bewildered one.
You of foolish resolve,
memorizing and reciting
the rules of grammar
is no match for death.
At the appointed time
rote
discipline
will not free you.

Do not crow
of youth, wealth,
or following.
Time steals all this—
in an instant.
Abandon
illusion.
Give yourself
only to knowing
the Lord's
feet.

11

Love the Lord, love the Lord.
The Lord—
love him, bewildered one.
You of foolish resolve,
memorizing and reciting
the rules of grammar
is no match for death.
At the appointed time
rote
discipline
will not free you.

Day and
night, dawn
and dusk,
spring
and winter
revolve.
Time
is amused,
as life
ebbs.
Still,
the bonds
of desire
do not
slacken. 12

Love the Lord, love the Lord.
The Lord—
love him, bewildered one.
You of foolish resolve,
memorizing and reciting
the rules of grammar
is no match for death.
At the appointed time
rote
discipline
will not free you.

Crazy fool,
why worry
that the one you
desire
or your prized
possessions
are gone?
Are they not given
to be renounced?
There is nothing
in the three worlds
that matters—
except truth.
Keep the company
of fervent
seekers and
awakened ones.
These companions
are the raft
that will carry
you across
the river of sorrows. 13

Love the Lord, love the Lord.
The Lord—
love him, bewildered one.
You of foolish resolve,
memorizing and reciting
the rules of grammar
is no match for death.
At the appointed time
rote
discipline
will not free you.

Ascetics may be of
shaven head
or matted lock,
with their cloth
scrubbed clean against
rock. Even so,
their gaze is like
stone.
They see not.
They are as foolish as any.
Their dress is a costume. 14

Love the Lord, love the Lord.
The Lord—
love him, bewildered one.
You of foolish resolve,
memorizing and reciting
the rules of grammar
is no match for death.
At the appointed time
rote
discipline
will not free you.

Of weak limb,
bald head,
and toothless gum,
an old man holds
only
to his staff.
Even so, the grip
of desire
does not
slacken. 15

Love the Lord, love the Lord.
The Lord—
love him, bewildered one.
You of foolish resolve,
memorizing and reciting
the rules of grammar
is no match for death.
At the appointed time
rote
discipline
will not free you.

Homeless,
with only a fire
for comfort at night,
with the sun's luster
behind him,
the seeker rests
chin
on
knees.
This kneeling beggar
of open palm
calls a tree
his shelter.
Even so,
the grip of desire
does not slacken. 16

Love the Lord, love the Lord.
The Lord—
love him, bewildered one.
You of foolish resolve,
memorizing and reciting
the rules of grammar
is no match for death.
At the appointed time
rote
discipline
will not free you.

Washing free
of sin,
upholding vows,
and giving,
a seeker may still
lack heart.
No one will find freedom
without devotion,
though born
a hundred
times over. 17

Love the Lord, love the Lord.
The Lord—
love him, bewildered one.
You of foolish resolve,
memorizing and reciting
the rules of grammar
is no match for death.
At the appointed time
rote
discipline
will not free you.

Dwelling in a temple
or at the foot of a tree
is all the same
to one who,
having renounced
possession and pleasure,
wrapped in deerskin,
sleeps on the earth.
Who would not be joyful
having realized
such
dispassion? 18

Love the Lord, love the Lord.
The Lord—
love him, bewildered one.
You of foolish resolve,
memorizing and reciting
the rules of grammar
is no match for death.
At the appointed time
rote
discipline
will not free you.

One may desire
austerity or pleasure,
companionship
or solitude,
but only one who
delights
in knowing
the Lord
rejoices, rejoices,
is ever joyful. 19

Love the Lord, love the Lord.
The Lord—
love him, bewildered one.
You of foolish resolve,
memorizing and reciting
the rules of grammar
is no match for death.
At the appointed time
rote
discipline
will not free you.

Contemplate any verse
of the *Bhagavad Gita.*
Sip
but a drop
of Ganges water.
One who knows
the play of the Lord,
one who worships
in this way,
need not
fear death.

Love the Lord, love the Lord.
The Lord—
love him, bewildered one.
You of foolish resolve,
memorizing and reciting
the rules of grammar
is no match for death.
At the appointed time
rote
discipline
will not free you.

Again and again,
we are born to die.
We seek the comfort
of the mother's womb.
Here and everywhere,
it is difficult to
break the cycle
of sorrows.
Lord,
in your grace,
carry me. 21

Love the Lord, love the Lord.
The Lord—
love him, bewildered one.
You of foolish resolve,
memorizing and reciting
the rules of grammar
is no match for death.
At the appointed time
rote
discipline
will not free you.

One who roams in rags,
following the sun,
may be of much
or no merit,
may be
without companion,
though in union
with conscious ecstasy.
This one appears perhaps
as a drunkard, a madman,
or a child. 22

Love the Lord, love the Lord.
The Lord—
love him, bewildered one.
You of foolish resolve,
memorizing and reciting
the rules of grammar
is no match for death.
At the appointed time
rote
discipline
will not free you.

Who are you? Who am I?
From where did you come?
Who is my mother?
Who is my father?
Having left aside
all things of this world,
consider it to be
like a dream. 23

Love the Lord, love the Lord.
The Lord—
love him, bewildered one.
You of foolish resolve,
memorizing and reciting
the rules of grammar
is no match for death.
At the appointed time
rote
discipline
will not free you.

The Lord is
within you,
and within me.
Everywhere
is the Lord.
You without patience—
your excitement
in seeking
is nonsense.
Be even-tempered
always,
if you wish to
know the Lord. 24

Love the Lord, love the Lord.
The Lord—
love him, bewildered one.
You of foolish resolve,
memorizing and reciting
the rules of grammar
is no match for death.
At the appointed time
rote
discipline
will not free you.

Don't strive to
discern enemies
from friends.
Don't cling to close relations.
See the Lord in all alike. 25

Love the Lord, love the Lord.
The Lord—
love him, bewildered one.
You of foolish resolve,
memorizing and reciting
the rules of grammar
is no match for death.
At the appointed time
rote
discipline
will not free you.

One who leaves aside
lust, fury, and greed,
all worldly
enchantment,
sees the truth in all.
Inquire into your
true nature,
for one without
experience of truth
lives in quiet
torment. 26

Love the Lord, love the Lord.
The Lord—
love him, bewildered one.
You of foolish resolve,
memorizing and reciting
the rules of grammar
is no match for death.
At the appointed time
rote
discipline
will not free you.

Sing the song
of the Lord.
Chant his
thousand names.
Meditate
upon his blessed form.
Let the wise lead.
Give the wealth of truth
to the miserable,
downtrodden,
and afflicted. 27

Love the Lord, love the Lord.
The Lord—
love him, bewildered one.
You of foolish resolve,
memorizing and reciting
the rules of grammar
is no match for death.
At the appointed time
rote
discipline
will not free you.

Sickness is sure to follow
one who seeks happiness
in the charms
of carnal pleasure.
In this world,
death is
the only guarantee.
Still one of
muddled mind
does not turn
from vice. 28

Love the Lord, love the Lord.
The Lord—
love him, bewildered one.
You of foolish resolve,
memorizing and reciting
the rules of grammar
is no match for death.
At the appointed time
rote
discipline
will not free you.

Wealth is worth little,
for it is not eternal.
Possessions bring
not even the slightest
hint of joy.
What's more,
one who is rich fears
cunning
offspring.
This is the way of the world. 29

Love the Lord, love the Lord.
The Lord—
love him, bewildered one.
You of foolish resolve,
memorizing and reciting
the rules of grammar
is no match for death.
At the appointed time
rote
discipline
will not free you.

Harness the life force.
Turn your attention
within.
Know truth from
what is not.
Seek truth.
Whisper prayers.
Merge with silence.
Do this with care.
Do this with great care. 30

Love the Lord, love the Lord.
The Lord—
love him, bewildered one.
You of foolish resolve,
memorizing and reciting
the rules of grammar
is no match for death.
At the appointed time
rote
discipline
will not free you.

Ardent seeker,
take refuge in
the lotus feet
of the *guru.*
Soon,
you will be free of
endless sorrow.
Control the senses
and the mind.
You will awaken
to the Lord,
who abides in the heart. 31

Love the Lord, love the Lord.
The Lord—
love him, bewildered one.
You of foolish resolve,
memorizing and reciting
the rules of grammar
is no match for death.
At the appointed time
rote
discipline
will not free you.

—*Sri Sankaracarya*

Notes

Verses 1-13 are attributed to Sri Sankaracarya, as are the concluding verses 28-31. Verses 14-27 are said to have been composed by the fourteen disciples who were with him that day in Kashi. It is said that the group came upon an aging *pandit* who was doggedly repeating grammatical rules for the sake of mere intellectual accomplishment. So, Sri Sankaracarya and his disciples began to sing of the glory of devotion to the Lord. *Bhaja Govindam.* The hymn is also known as *Moha Mudgar*a. This title compares it to a hammer that, with its ringing refrain, shatters delusion.

Madhurastakam

His mouth is sweet, his face is sweet,
his glance is sweet, his laugh is sweet,
his heart is sweet, his saunter sweet.
My sweet Lord is all that is sweet. 1

His words are sweet, his deeds are sweet,
his cloth is sweet, his *mudras* sweet,
his absence sweet, his wanderings sweet.
My sweet Lord is all that is sweet. 2

His flute is sweet, the riversands sweet,
His touch is sweet, his feet are sweet,
His dance is sweet, his friendship sweet,
My sweet Lord is all that is sweet. 3

His song is sweet, his shawl is sweet,
His meals are sweet, his sleep is sweet,
His shape is sweet, his musk smudge sweet.
My sweet Lord is all that is sweet. 4

His grace is sweet, his name is sweet,
this thief is sweet, his charm is sweet,
his *betel* quid sweet, his promise is sweet.
My sweet Lord is all that is sweet. 5

His berries are sweet, his garland is sweet,
his river is sweet, her ripples are sweet,
his swimming is sweet, the lotus is sweet,
My sweet Lord is all that is sweet. 6

The milkmaids are sweet, their antics are sweet,
to be one is sweet, and freedom is sweet—
the desire is sweet, the detachment is sweet.
My sweet Lord is all that is sweet. 7

This cowherd is sweet, his cows are sweet,
his switch is sweet, all creation is sweet,
the ripening is sweet, the fruit is sweet
freedom.
My sweet Lord is all that is sweet. 8

—*Sri Vallabhacarya*

Hanuman Chalisa

I take refuge in the dust of the guru's holy feet
to polish the mirror of the heart.
So, I prepare to sing the glories
of the father of the Raghu dynasty.
Devotion bestows all that is good in life:
virtue, prosperity, joy, and freedom.

I am not learned,
but I supplicate the great Hanuman
to bless me in these efforts.
Son of the wind,
flood me with courage, intelligence,
and your eternal grace,
so that I may praise you
with all my heart.
I offer to you my sorrows and failings.

Hail to the feet of Sita's Lord Ram.

Victory to you, Hanuman, ocean of light.
Victory to the monkey king,
who is adored through
time and space,
mind and dream,
and that which can never
be known.
Carrying Ram's message,
you are the hero of all time.
None are as strong as you,
son of Anjani,
you who are called child of the wind. 1-2

Hanuman, you are strong and fearless,
like a sudden bolt of lightning.
Your light relieves the mind
of its sufferings.
You are a faithful companion,
the most desirable company. 3

Strong, and adorned with splendid silks,
bright earrings, and long, curly locks,
you glow, golden with the light of compassion. 4

You wield mace and flag,
and wear a simple,
sacred thread
across your shoulders.
Son of the chief, the lion-hearted one,
you are the boon bestowed by Lord Siva. 5-6

You are the wellspring
of wisdom, wit, and virtue,
so humbly devoted to Lord Ram. 7

Drinking in the stories
of your beloved Lord
like nectar,
you live forever
in the hearts of Sri Ram,
his brother Lakshman,
and his wife, Mother Sita. 8

In tiny form, you humbled yourself
before Queen Sita.
Before the demon ruler, you appeared
with great force
and burnt his city, Lanka,
to the ground. 9

In wrathful form you slew
the demon army,
as heartfelt service
to the Lord of righteousness. 10

You procured the elixir of life,
sacred mountain herb,
to revive Lakshman, and so,
Lord Ram embraced you.
"You are like my own kin," he said,
"a brother to me.
Forever, may thousands
praise your name." 11-12

Of the countless saints and sages,
gods, scholars, and poets,
none can tell of
your limitless glory.
Not Sanaka, Brahma, Narada, Sarada,
or even Lord Vishnu's serpent throne. 13-14

Still, they praise you.
The Lords of death and wealth.
The wind, She sings your name
from all directions. 15

You served Sugriva, a leader of your tribe,
bringing him before Lord Ram
who then named him king. 16

Vibhishana, brother of the demon king,
revered your word, and so
ruled over Lanka. 17

You leapt a thousand miles
up to the sun
and swallowed it,
like a sweet,
golden fruit.
In your mouth, you carried Lord Ram's ring
and leapt easily across the ocean.
Nothing is impossible
with your ever-flowing grace. 18-20

You are the keeper of Lord Ram's door.
None may enter without your grace. 21

You are the refuge of all blessings.
Those who love you know no fear.
Only you radiate such glory.
The universe trembles
at the sound of your voice. 22

Ghosts, demons, and
troublesome spirits
shudder and disband
when your name is called. 23-24

Nor can pain or illness
withstand the sound. 25

One who thinks only of you,
whose every breath
and act of service
is in your name
will be forever freed. 26

Ram embodies righteousness.
You bring his word to life.
Whoever bows down before you,
seeking from the heart,
is blessed
with utter and eternal
fulfillment. 27-28

Your glory lights the ages of
gold, silver, bronze, and iron.
The breath of the universe
is the sound of your name. 29

You protect tradition, guardian of *sadhus*,
destroyer of demons,
sweetest devotee of Lord Ram. 30

The eight *siddhis* and nine *nidhis*,
all power and treasure,
are yours to grant,
by the blessed boon of Mother Sita. 31

You heal with the elixir
of Lord Ram's name.
Forever will you remain devoted,
lifting the burdens
of true and helpless seekers,
lifetime after lifetime. 32

In singing your praises,
one is reunited with Lord Ram,
relieved of countless sufferings,
and of future rebirth.
Such a one, at death,
will go either to the glorious city of Lord Ram,
or be reborn in this world
as his most humble servant. 33-34

One need think of nothing else,
for dearest Hanuman,
you bestow all delight. 35

Pain and suffering vanish
when your strength and glory
are remembered. 36

Yes! Yes! Yes! Lord Hanuman is victorious.
Let your grace flood through me,
glorious *guru.* 37

One who sings from memory
these verses
one hundred times
is freed from meaningless desire,
discovering within the greatest joy. 38

One who recites these verses daily
will be blessed with perfection,
as Lord Siva is witness. 39

Tulsidas, the eternal servant of beloved Hari, says,
"Lord, forever, make your home in my heart." 40

Son of the wind,
destroyer of sorrows,
embodiment of all blessings,
With Lord Ram, Lakshman, and Mother Sita,
live enshrined in my heart.

—*Sri Tulsidas*

Notes

This translation was written on Hanuman Jayanti, 2009. It has been reprinted with permission from literary journal *Lalitamba* (Issue 4; Chintamani Books, 2011).

Lingastakam

I bow to the sacred *lingam*
that is worshipped by the creator
and slayer of demons, alike.
Pure, praised, and resplendent,
victorious over embodied sorrow,
the destroyer of suffering—
to that *sada siva lingam*, I bow. 1

Adored by gods and sages,
burning desire to blessed ash,
cause of all compassion
destroyer of pride, arrogance, and conceit—
to that *sada siva lingam*, I bow. 2

Honored with fragrant balms
and perfumes,
turgid wisdom, perfect master,
praised even by the ignorant—
to that *sada siva lingam*, I bow. 3

Decorated with gold
ornaments and
enormous, glittering jewels,
enrobed in the coils
of the thick serpent king,
destroyer of pompous sacrifice—
to that *sada siva lingam*, I bow. 4

Smeared with saffron
and sandalwood paste,
lotus born of mud,
stealthy thief of sorrow,
pure effulgence,
the one who forgives all sin—
to that *sada siva lingam*, I bow. 5

Worshipped by multitudes
of holy and divine beings,
mood of devotion,
hope of the afflicted
most excellent radiance—
to that *sada siva lingam*, I bow. 6

Tantric *cakra*,
lotus of eight petals,
giver of life,
the one who uplifts the poor—
to that *sada siva lingam*, I bow. 7

Benevolent parent,
divine beloved,
Lord
forever worshipped with wild
and fragrant flowers,
immanent and transcendent being—
to that *sada siva lingam*, I bow. 8

One who reads, recites, or chants
these eight verses in praise of Lord Siva
and thinks always of Lord Shiva
merges with Lord Shiva, and
lives forever in delight with the Lord.

—These verses are attributed by some to Sri Sankaracarya.

Bhavanyastakam

No father, no mother,
or brother have I—
no relation, no child,
or loved one have I.
Mother, I am alone
in the world.
Even this mind,
with its victories
and intellect,
is somewhat confused
and cannot
be counted upon.
You alone, you alone
are my true refuge. 1

In seeking the highest
existence,
I have fallen.
Mother, I am drowning
in this ocean of sorrows,
and I am afraid.
I am caught in the noose
of my own lust and greed,
caught on the wheel
of birth and rebirth.
You alone, you alone
are my true refuge. 2

Mother, I have nothing to offer you.
I can't find you through meditation.
I know no sacred rituals,
verses of praise,
or even a single *mantra.*
In truth,
I don't know how to worship you,
though I need to feel your grace.
You alone, you alone
are my true refuge. 3

Mother, I don't deserve you, and
I have no one to guide me on this path.
I am not liberated or even absorbed in meditation.
I am not devoted to you as I should be.
I don't know how to keep vows.
You alone, you alone
are my true refuge. 4

Mother, though I try hard
my deeds are flawed.
I am bereft of spiritual friends.
I am not a scholar,
nor am I humble enough
to serve you.
I have been accepted
by no teacher.
I am confused and clingy,
and I often say the wrong thing.
My gaze is unsteady.
You alone, you alone
are my true refuge. 5

Mother, I know nothing of divine
beings. Sometimes, I don't feel
respect, delight, awe, compassion,
or even devotion. No, I don't
know much of these things.
I am just your child.
You alone, you alone
are my true refuge. 6

In the throes of quarrel or lust,
when I fall reckless
or leave you,
when I am hurt,
when there is no caring
face to turn to,
in desert or in wilderness,
Mother, protect me.
Always hold me close.
You alone, you alone
are my true refuge. 7

Mother, I am a beggar—
an orphan. I am afraid
of disease and old age.
Yes, I am afflicted with
sorrow. I feel
vulnerable.
The world seems cold.
When I am lost,
the only truth is you.
You alone, you alone
are my true refuge. 8

—*Sri Sankaracarya*

Mahisasura Mardini Stotram

Dear daughter of the mountain
who makes the earth fertile
and delights the universe,
you who roam low hills
even as you dwell on the peak,
playmate of Vishnu,
victorious Goddess,
wife of the blue-throated Lord,
mother to all—*Victory to you!*
You conquer the buffalo demon with ease,
wearing your hair in a pleasing braid,
sweet daughter of the mountain. 1

Dear daughter of the mountain
who rains blessings on the gods,
tames the unruly,
and is patient with the foul-mouthed,
you bring all joys. Daughter of abundance,
you are Lord Siva's contentment.
You plunder faults,
even as you respond
to cries of distress.
Courageous girl
who defeats anger and arrogance,
you worship like a flooding river—*Victory to you!*
You conquer the buffalo demon with ease,
wearing your hair in a pleasing braid,
sweet daughter of the mountain. 2

Universal mother,
rapturous mother,
fragrant orange blossom,
beloved who laughs aloud
in the midst of the forest,
crest jewel,
Himalayan peak,
taste of honey,
sweet one who defeats demons,
you worship and rejoice—*Victory to you!*
You conquer the buffalo demon with ease,
wearing your hair in a pleasing braid,
sweet daughter of the mountain. 3

Dear daughter
who cracks the skulls of the ignorant,
you behead those swollen with pride. Riding
the noble lion that crouches and springs,
you are courageous.
You push through elephant
cheeks and trunks.
Immersed in battle,
you are alluring.
You leave in the dust
those of shaven head and staff.
Lord, warrior, and slave,
they are alike, to you.
You fracture class structure—*Victory to you!*
You conquer the buffalo demon with ease,
wearing your hair in a pleasing braid,
sweet daughter of the mountain. 4

Dear one of endless strength,
you delight in eradicating enemies—
drunken infatuation,
foolish pride,
bloated arrogance.
Young girl so charming,
you elicit support from
your Lord's attendant,
he who is skilled
and clever in battle.
He cuts through
the dangers of the field,
as well the weakness
of an ignorant mind—*Victory to you!*
You conquer the buffalo demon with ease,
wearing your hair in a pleasing braid,
sweet daughter of the mountain. 5

Dear daughter,
you give refuge to the enemy,
the hero, and the innocent,
alike. Your compassion
relieves the three worlds
of fear, even as you stand ready
to spear with your glance of grace
those embroiled in strife,
those whose ignorance
brings pain. Fiery one,
passionate girl,
you are enlivened
by the drumbeat of your Lord.
You are like a thunderbolt—*Victory to you!*
You conquer the buffalo demon with ease,
wearing your hair in a pleasing braid,
sweet daughter of the mountain. 6

Dear one who
exhales primordial sound,
elemental *mantra*,
girl of smoky eyes
you eradicate sin with a sidelong glance.
You are a blood red jewel. You are
the flowering vine that revives your Lord.
He is satisfied by such great acts
as your slaying the demons of duality—*Victory to you!*
You conquer the buffalo demon with ease,
wearing your hair in a pleasing braid,
sweet daughter of the mountain. 7

Dearest, you dance and shiver
at the moment before battle,
your limbs adorned with
all manner of ornament.
Holding bow in hand,
you pull arrows
from a quiver
of burnished gold
to fell fearsome
mountain warriors.
Battle is no more
than a colorful play to you,
such joyous drama—*Victory to you!*
You conquer the buffalo demon with ease,
wearing your hair in a pleasing braid,
sweet daughter of the mountain. 8

Victory to soft
prayers of surrender.
Victory. Victory
to loud cries of your
highest praise.
The universe is utterly devoted to you
whose tinkling anklets
infatuate the Lord
with whom you dance
until the world
disappears,
reappears,
disappears.
You delight in the play
of song and dance—*Victory to you!*
You conquer the buffalo demon with ease,
wearing your hair in a pleasing braid,
sweet daughter of the mountain. 9

Darling blossom,
sweet blossom,
blossom, you enchant the mind.
Your loveliness shines in the darkness,
like the full moon illuminating the night.
You are resplendent.
Your gentle glance attracts
devotees and the Lord alike,
as if they were black bees,
buzzing bees,
bees seeking nectar.
Sweet flower—*Victory to you!*
You conquer the buffalo demon with ease,
wearing your hair in a pleasing braid,
sweet daughter of the mountain. 10

In the company of strong men,
you wage war
you so vulnerable, like a deer.
You are the delight of heroes.
You live amongst the jasmine blossoms
and dance to the cricket's song.
You shine in the darkness of night,
like the moon of spring tide,
coquettish,
with face half-veiled.
At dawn, you blossom.
Tender virgin,
beautiful goddess Lalita—*Victory to you!*
You conquer the buffalo demon with ease,
wearing your hair in a pleasing braid,
sweet daughter of the mountain. 11

With thighs like elephant cheeks,
your cries are rapturous music.
Leader of elephant herds,
lustrous ornament of the three worlds,
the Lord's most precious jewel,
you are the fullness of the moon.
Affectionate girl,
you give bountifully,
yet you excite desire.
You are as bewildering
as the scent of jasmine.
You agitate the mind—*Victory to you!*
You conquer the buffalo demon with ease,
wearing your hair in a pleasing braid,
sweet daughter of the mountain. 12

Dear daughter,
the purity of the lotus petal is yours.
You of melodious murmur
and gentle brow,
you who sport and play with swans,
you are graceful.
Like the waterlily,
you reveal
your delicate splendor
in the moonlight.
Devotees throng to you,
as bees swarm
to the flowering tree.
Blossom
of intoxicating breath—*Victory to you!*
You conquer the buffalo demon with ease,
wearing your hair in a pleasing braid,
sweet daughter of the mountain. 13

Dear daughter,
the call of your flute
shames the nightingale's song.
You are to be found in the mountains,
amongst those whose cry
is primitive.
You are captivating,
cavorting with
the wildest women,
who soon
reflect your refinement—*Victory to you!*
You conquer the buffalo demon with ease,
wearing your hair in a pleasing braid,
sweet daughter of the mountain. 14

Darling daughter
with hips wrapped in yellow silk,
your curves
are shimmering hillocks.
Such radiance brings the moon to shine.
Simple girl,
your toenails are like the moon,
reflecting the diadem light
of kings and gods
who bow to take refuge there.
All find strength at your tender feet—*Victory to you!*
You conquer the buffalo demon with ease,
wearing your hair in a pleasing braid,
sweet daughter of the mountain. 15

You outshine the sun of a thousand rays.
More brilliant than a thousand suns,
you are praised by the rays of a thousand suns.
You liberate the gods.
Luminous savior.
shining protector,
splendid charioteer,
you turn all toward *samadhi.*
You are *samadhi.*
You proclaim aloud all that is beautiful.
Samadhi! Samadhi! Samadhi!—Victory to you!
You conquer the buffalo demon with ease,
wearing your hair in a pleasing braid,
sweet daughter of the mountain. 16

At your lotus feet,
all compassion resides.
You are the source of bliss
and all that is blessed.
You in whom the lotus dwells,
you who sit
upon the full-blown lotus,
if I were to surrender
completely
at your feet,
at your holy feet,
would there be anything left
to realize?—*Victory to you!*
You conquer the buffalo demon with ease,
wearing your hair in a pleasing braid,
sweet daughter of the mountain. 17

Darling daughter,
your form is worshipped
with light, sandalwood,
melodious song,
and holy water,
yet you are the spacious sky.
Whoever is intimate
with your breasts,
full like pitchers,
experiences sweet bliss.
One who bows down
to take refuge at your feet,
finds eternal life.
Your feet are the abode
of the Lord—*Victory to you!*
You conquer the buffalo demon with ease,
wearing your hair in a pleasing braid,
sweet daughter of the mountain. 18

Dear one of radiant face,
you who are praised by all,
I yearn to be loved as your very own.
You of face like the stainless moon,
you of sweet countenance,
would you turn away from my plea?
You are indeed my mother.
You are the one whose name
the Lord calls.
Shed your grace
upon me, too—*Victory to you!*
You conquer the buffalo demon with ease,
wearing your hair in a pleasing braid,
sweet daughter of the mountain. 19

Sweet child who overflows
with compassion for the sorrowful,
flood me with your grace.
Dear mother of all being,
in your mercy,
let me call you my mother.
Please smile upon this supplicant,
though I am not selfless enough
to love you as I should,
for it is you who remove
all affliction—*Victory to you!*
You conquer the buffalo demon with ease,
wearing your hair in a pleasing braid,
sweet daughter of the mountain. 20

—*Sri Sankaracarya*